My Friend Leslie

My Friend Leslie

The Story of a Handicapped Child

by *MAXINE B. ROSENBERG*

photographs by GEORGE ANCONA

Lothrop, Lee & Shepard Books/New York

The author wishes to thank the Parsons family for their cooperation and support in making this book possible. Special thanks also go to Florence Klein and the Briarcliff, New York, school system.

*Text copyright © 1983 by Maxine B. Rosenberg.
Photographs copyright © 1983 by George Ancona. All rights
reserved. No part of this book may be reproduced or utilized
in any form or by any means, electronic or mechanical,
including photocopying, recording or by any information
storage and retrieval system, without permission in
writing from the Publisher. Inquiries should be addressed
to Lothrop, Lee & Shepard Books, a division of William
Morrow & Company, Inc., 105 Madison Avenue, New York,
New York 10016.
Printed in the United States of America.
First Edition
1 2 3 4 5 6 7 8 9 10*

*Library of Congress Cataloging in Publication Data
Rosenberg, Maxine B.
My Friend Leslie.
Summary: Presents a multi-handicapped kindergarten
child, who is well-accepted by her classmates, in various
situations within the school setting.
1. Leslie. 2. Physically handicapped children—United
States—Biography—Juvenile literature.
[1. Physically handicapped] I. Ancona, George, ill.
II. Title.
RD796.L47R67 1983   362.4 [B]   82-12734
ISBN 0-688-01690-1
ISBN 0-688-01691-X (lib. bdg.)*

To Paul, with much love.
And to Mark, David, Seth, and Karin.
                                    –M.B.R.

Leslie and I have been friends for a long time. My name is Karin,

but she calls me "Froggie." Leslie likes to tell jokes to make me laugh.

This year Leslie and I are in the same kindergarten, and we ride to school together. Since Leslie is so little, her mommy boosts her onto the bus.

"Where are you sitting?" Leslie calls to me loudly. Out goes my hand, and she finds me.

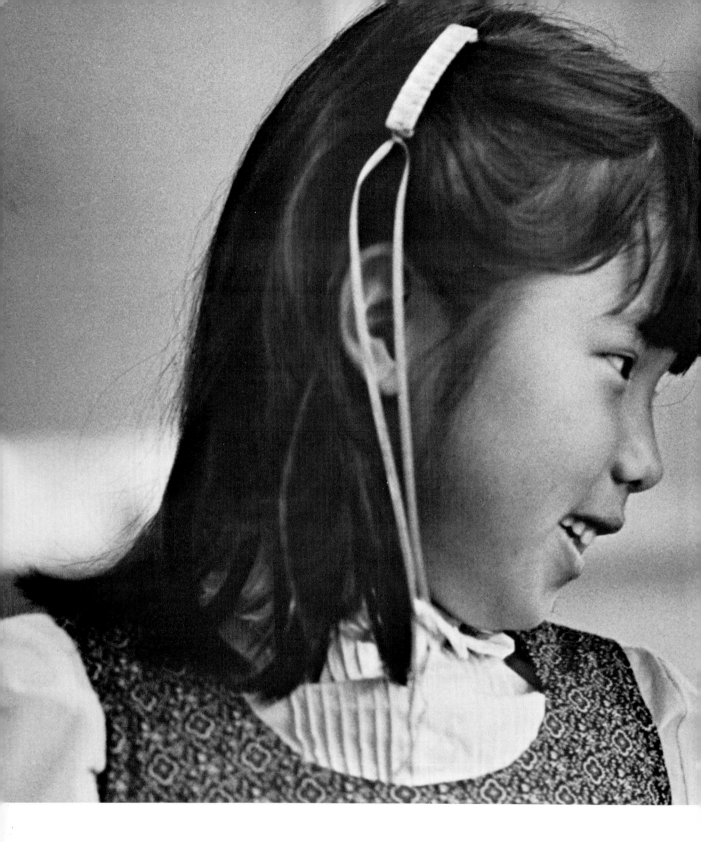

Leslie has trouble with her eyes and doesn't see clearly unless things are up close. That's just the way she was born. Sometimes,

when we're talking, she leans so near to look at me that her face
touches mine. Then we both begin to giggle and we clunk heads.

Leslie was also born with a hearing problem. She couldn't understand anyone who didn't speak in a loud voice. So now she wears two hearing aids, one in each ear. They are attached to the ends of a headband and work like microphones, making sounds louder.

When I talk to Leslie now, I never have to yell anymore for her to hear me. But if I whisper, she says my voice is too soft. So we go behind the bookshelves, where nobody can hear us, and I speak a little louder. Then she tells me a secret, too, in her deep voice.

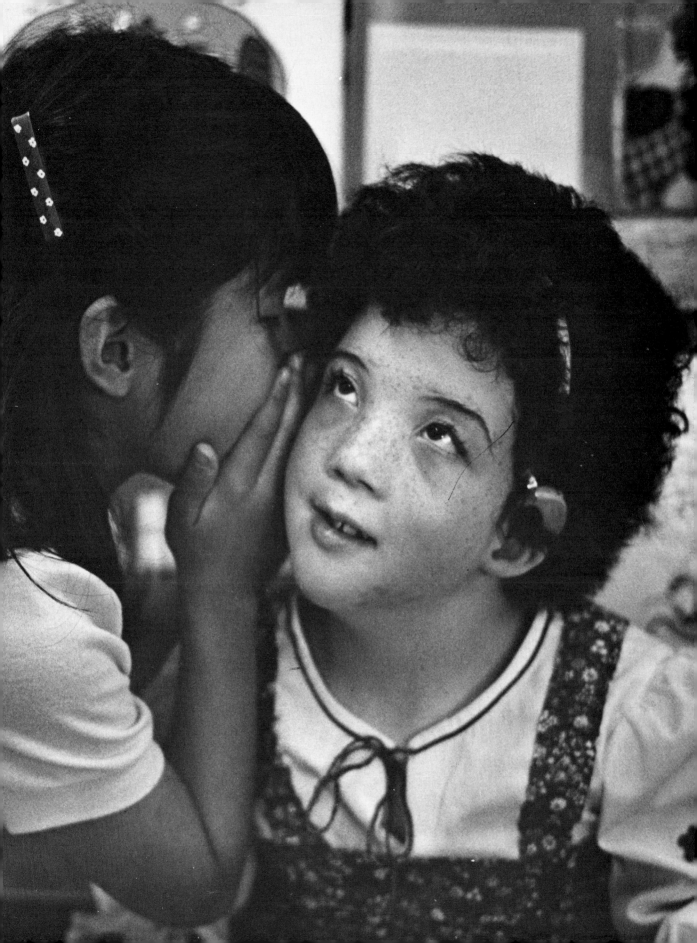

I remember the first day of school. Everyone in the class stared at Leslie. They wondered about those things in her ears and why she moved closer whenever someone talked.

Ms. Klein, our teacher, explained about Leslie's eyes and ears. She said that sometimes Leslie has trouble moving, too, and she might need our help. So we started bringing Leslie her paper and crayons, and we even carried her around.

Then Ms. Klein said that Leslie didn't need *that* much help. She was right. Even though Leslie is handicapped, she can do almost everything for herself. It just takes her a little longer than some people.

When we paint together,
Leslie puts on her own
smock. But I button it for her,
because she can't move her
fingers and hands easily. She
was born with stiff muscles
that don't stretch like rubber
bands, as most people's do.

It's also hard for Leslie to turn the faucet on and off when she changes the paint water. That doesn't stop her, though. She goes back and forth to the sink, emptying and filling the cups. She likes her brushes to be clean. So do I.

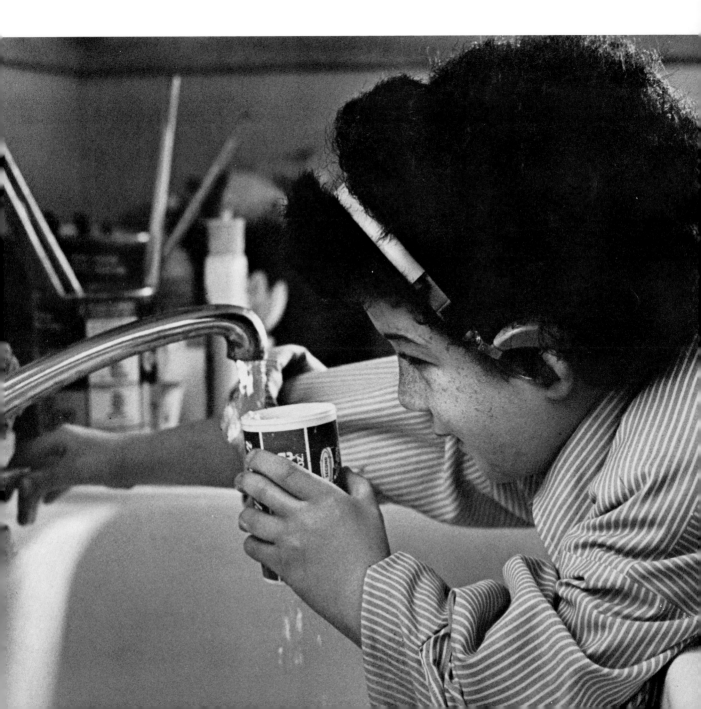

Red and green. Those are Leslie's favorite colors. She puts her face up to the cans to find out which is which. Then she usually paints a flower, bigger than anyone else's.

Sometimes Leslie
moves so close to see
her picture that a red
smudge lands on her
nose. If I tell her she
looks like a circus
clown, she takes her
brush and tries to
make me her twin.

When Ms. Klein calls, "Music time," we sit on a special
rug and learn a new song. Ms. Klein plays the piano
softly and sings to us in a low voice.

If Leslie is too far away, she jumps up and stamps her feet. "Louder, louder," she shouts. "I can't hear." I'm always afraid she might cry.

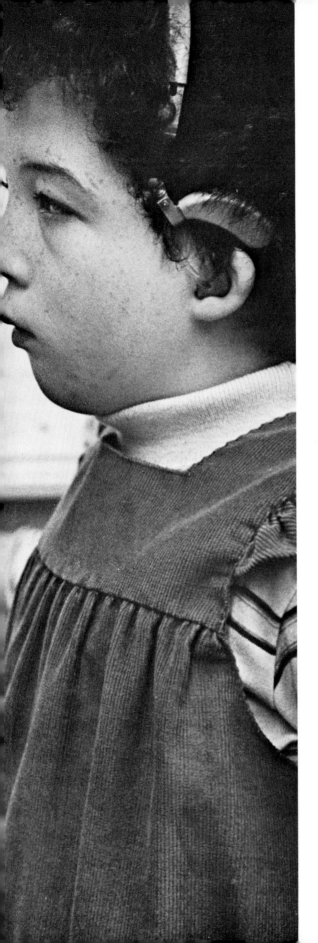

Then our teacher says, "Come up closer, Leslie." Standing next to Ms. Klein, Leslie watches the teacher's mouth carefully and lipreads the words. She puts her hands on the piano, too, and smiles. She says the sound vibrations tickle. When Leslie starts swaying to the rhythm of the music, everyone else starts swaying with her.

Sometimes our class makes soup or stew. Leslie and I work together and share a vegetable peeler. But first Leslie likes to feel the onions, carrots, and potatoes. Then she guesses what they are by their smell. I think she has a nose like a rabbit!

Peeling the onions always makes us cry. We run to the water fountain and wash away the sting.

In our class, we take turns doing many jobs. Everyone wants to be "Child of the Week." That means you can walk down the hallway alone, bringing messages to other classrooms.

When it's Leslie's turn, I get to go with her because she needs someone to show her the way. It's fun to go through the school by ourselves. Some days we peek into the library or ask the art teacher for extra clay.

One time we had a message for Leslie's brother's fourth grade teacher. When Leslie saw her brother, she shouted, "Hi, Greg!"

I told her, "Be quiet," but she didn't listen.

Even more than being
"Child of the Week," Leslie
likes to read. And no wonder!
She is the best reader in the
class. I can read a few words,
but she can read a whole
story. Her favorite is *Little
Red Riding Hood,* and Ms.
Klein lets her read it aloud
to us.

Leslie holds the book close.
She could wear her glasses to
make the words look bigger.
But she says they bother her
and that she sees better with
her face near the page.

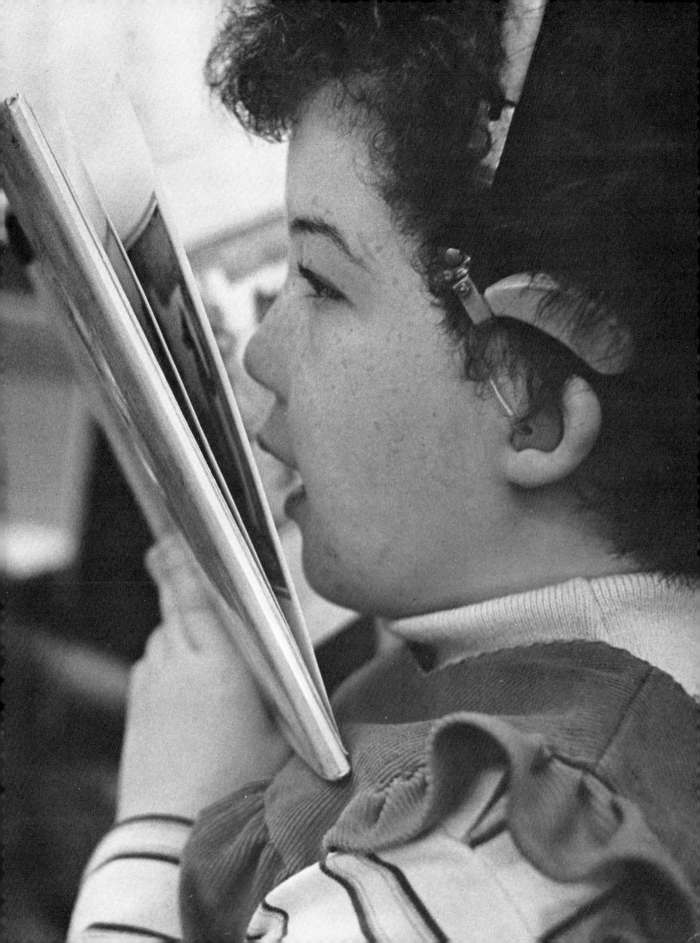

Leslie acts out the different parts of the story. First she speaks in a deep voice so we think she's the wolf. Then she pretends she is Little Red Riding Hood and talks in a high, squeaky voice. We try to be quiet, but Leslie is so funny we can't help laughing.

When she is finished, everyone claps. Leslie takes a bow, almost touching her toes.

Leslie is good at touching her toes. In gym, she can do it ten times in a row. She is also good at twirling around like an airplane and growing tall like a flower.

But if we climb the ropes, Leslie needs help. Her stiff muscles make it hard for her to cling to the rope with her hands and feet. So Mrs. Kramer, our gym teacher, boosts Leslie to a big knot. She holds on to her while Leslie swings.

On sunny days
we go outside.
Leslie and I love
the merry-go-round
best. She sits in
the middle so she
won't topple off.
We both scream
when it goes fast.

One day our class took a trip to a nature center. At first Leslie was unhappy and wanted to go home. The prairie dogs and porcupines were too far back in their cages for her to see. She couldn't find the gray snake that was lying near the rock, either. Finally, she sat down on the ground and wouldn't take another step.

I didn't know what to do. Then Ms. Klein said, "Lunchtime," and Leslie jumped up to be the first in line. We ate our picnic lunch under a tall tree. During dessert, Leslie stuck the watermelon pits on her cheeks and said she had chicken pox.

After lunch we went wading in the
nearby brook. The water was so cold!

Leslie splashed me with her toes, and
I laughed so much my stomach hurt.

By the time we rode the bus home, my shorts and shirt were dripping wet, but I didn't care.

"It was a great trip," Leslie said to me, yawning. Before I could say yes, her head was on my shoulder.

I thought Leslie must like having a good friend like me. I know how lucky I am to have a good friend like Leslie.

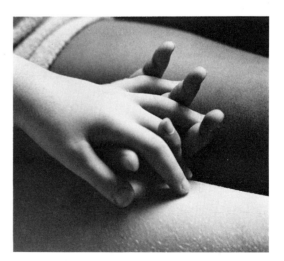

Leslie Parsons is only one of the more than two million handicapped children in this country who have been mainstreamed in public schools. The general causes of these children's disabilities are maternal infections (such as rubella), drugs or X-rays, genetic aberrations, and medical complications during pregnancy and delivery. Sometimes the cause is unknown, as in Leslie's case.

The second Parsons child, Leslie was born with a visual impairment (she is legally blind), moderate hearing loss, cleft palate, muscular imperfection in her extremities, and ptosis of the eyelids. Special physical therapy began when Leslie was three months old. By her first birthday, she was enrolled in a school program, funded by the federal government and the D.C. [District of Columbia] Society, that consisted of speech, language, and physical therapy. This early intensive education was, Mrs. Parsons feels, largely responsible for bringing Leslie on a par with other children her age.

Currently in the third grade, Leslie still has some difficulty with tasks requiring muscle coordination and fine motor skills, as well as visual acuity. She wears a hearing aid, for which she is refitted periodically to accommodate her growth, and has prescribed glasses, although she chooses not to use them. Every few years, she requires an operation to reduce the fluid in her ears, and last year she required a second operation to tighten the muscles in her eyelids (the first took place when she was three).

Twice a week Leslie works with a teacher of the visually impaired. Through the use of a new device that enlarges and projects print onto a screen, Leslie can read and write independently with less eyestrain. An outstanding reader and stand-up comedienne, ebullient Leslie says she wants to be a ballerina when she grows up.